GIN OF THRONES

GIN OF THRONES

Cocktails and Drinking Games Inspired by the World of Westeros

MAESTER JAGER

PRION

This is published by
Prion Books
an imprint of Carlton
Books Ltd
20 Mortimer Street
London W1T 3JW
Copyright © 2019 Carlton
Books Ltd

10 8 6 4 2 1 3 5 7 9

A CIP catalogue for this
book is available from the
British Library.

ISBN 978-1-91161-028-1

Printed in China

CONTENTS

INTRODUCTION

GATHER AROUND, fellow *Game of Thrones* fans. It's time to tell you a story. A story of ice and fire(ball), an epic tale that's filled with dragons, knights, heroes, villains and enough hooch to floor the entire Seven Kingdoms.

Welcome to *Gin of Thrones*, a carefully curated compendium of cocktails inspired by Westeros and the characters that inhabit it. From the Maesters of Oldtown to the barflies of Flea Bottom we've scoured the Seven Kingdoms, and beyond, to put together a library of libations based on the hit HBO TV series and the George R. R. Martin novels that inspired it.

If you're a hardcore fan (the kind of person who knows their Highgarden from their High Valyrian, who's read the books, watched the shows and plotted out the full Targaryen family tree in the process), this is the cocktail guide for you.

However, if you're the kind of person who knows less than Jon Snow, that's fine too. Everyone is welcome here. **Just be warned that there are spoilers ahead**, so if you're planning to enjoy the action first-hand, go and read the books or watch the TV shows right now. No, seriously, what are you waiting for? Do it. Now. OK, you're back. Ready? Let's continue.

There are eight chapters, each of which cover one TV season and contain a heady mix of cocktails inspired by the prominent events and characters in those episodes. From fruity

numbers that are perfect for a summer evening in Sunspear to hearty fare that's sure to warm even the coldest of White Walker hearts, we've got something for everyone. In fact, keep reading and you're guaranteed to find a cocktail to suit every taste.

For Stark bannermen we have libations like the Bran(dy) Alexander, a delicious drink with all the bite of a direwolf on a cold Winterfell morning. For those who like their cups full and their purses heavy, we've got a boozy little number we like to call Shaken Not Lannistirred. Looking for something a little more exotic? Check out our Piña-Khal-Ada, or why not whip up some Fermented Mare's Milk for an authentic taste of Essos?

If all that booze has made you hungrier than one of Ramsay Bolton's hounds, worry not. We've cooked up a buffet of bar bites to satisfy even the most insatiable of appetites. From Unsullied Spiced Nuts and Theon's Cocktail Weenies to dishes that have nothing to do with male anatomy at all, there's a smorgasbord of snacks to soak up all the alcohol you're going to be drinking over the next 140 pages.

Finally, for hosts whose soirees are sorrier than a Frey family wedding, we've got drinking games that are guaranteed to liven up any party – as long as your guests are willing to down a shot every time a character dies on screen, that is.

So, to paraphrase Tyrion Lannister: get ready to drink and know things as we play the *Gin of Thrones*.

SEASON

1

SONG OF ICE AND FIRE(BALL)

B ACK IN 1991, George R. R. Martin could not have known the impact that his imagination would have on popular culture. The release of the first book in his *Song of Ice and Fire* series would not only go on to become a bestseller, but it would eventually spawn more than 6 sequels, a hit TV show and, a full 18 years later, the pun-tastic cocktail book you're reading right now!

It's a story that has come to define a generation – one that, at the time of writing, the man himself hasn't even finished scribbling yet. So, to help kick his imagination into high gear and set his fingers fluttering over the keyboard, we cooked up a guzzle-worthy shot that's guaranteed to shift writer's block faster than you can say: "Daenerys of the House Targaryen, the First of Her Name, the Unburnt, Queen of the Andals, the Rhoynar and the First Men, Queen of Meereen, Khaleesi of the Great Grass Sea, Protector of the Realm, Lady Regent of the Seven Kingdoms, Breaker of Chains and Mother of Dragons."

RECIPE

INGREDIENTS

1 oz Fireball cinnamon
  whiskey
1 oz crème de menthe
1 oz Irish cream liqueur

METHOD

1 Mix the ingredients in a cocktail shaker with ice.

2 Strain into a shot glass of your choice.

3 Down the hatch!

*"He is the prince that was promised,
and his is the song of ice and fire."*

—RHAEGAR TARGARYEN

BARATHEON BUCK'S FIZZ

Hands up – who misses the Baratheons? From Renly's showmanship to Stannis's stiff upper lip, the House of the Black Stag has given us some of the best characters to grace *Game of Thrones*. Head, shoulders and beer belly above the rest of the family, however, is King Robert himself – played brilliantly on the HBO show by Mark Addy.

A hard-drinking, tournament-loving womanizer who didn't so much sit on the Iron Throne as sway on it drunkenly, he's a poster boy for excess and a character who would probably sample every cocktail in this book and still have the energy to go hunt a wild boar for his dinner. We're not recommending you try anything like that at home, of course.

But in honour of Robert and the House Baratheon, you could sample our Baratheon Buck's Fizz – a cocktail fit for a king, especially one who likes to make a start on his imbibing as early as possible.

RECIPE

INGREDIENTS

1 1/2 oz champagne
1 1/2 oz freshly squeezed
orange juice
Orange twist, to garnish

METHOD

1 Add chilled orange juice to a
champagne flute.

2 Top with champagne.

3 Drink until you're too fat to fit into
your breastplate.

"I want the funeral feast to be
the biggest the kingdom ever saw,
and I want everyone to taste the
boar that got me."
—ROBERT BARATHEON

PIÑA-KHAL-ADA

THIS EXOTIC-SOUNDING tipple has been refreshing beach-based imbibers for decades, and for good reason. Heck, it's so famous that there was even a song written in its honour. How does it go again...?

"If you like Piña-Khal-adas, and ride your horse on the plains, If you're not into oceans, and wed the Breaker of Chains, If you're a legendary warrior, with a large Khalasar, Then beware of blood magic, coz it won't get you far."

"Che dothras che drivos."
—DOTHRAKI FOR "RIDE OR DIE"

RECIPE

INGREDIENTS

1 oz white rum
1 oz coconut cream (or
  fermented mare's
  milk if you want the
  genuine Dothraki
  experience)
3 oz pineapple juice
Crushed ice
Pineapple triangle, to
  garnish

METHOD

1 Mix all the ingredients (except for
  the garnish) with crushed ice in
  your cocktail shaker of choice.

2 Shake it like you're dancing at a
  Dothraki wedding.

3 Pour into a chilled glass, garnish
  and enjoy.

*"Yer Jalan Atthirari Anni.
(Moon of my life.)"*
—KHAL DROGO

INCEST BETWEEN THE SHEETS

THE LANNISTERS – we are told – always pay their debts. But it seems that they also always sleep with their siblings, or at least that's what we've learned after eight seasons of Cersei and Jaime's all-lion love-in. Although, as yucky as their relationship might be, they're not the only ones guilty of keeping things in the family.

Viserys had something of an unhealthy obsession with his sister, Craster's Keep was nothing if not creepy, Theon took a pass at Yara, and not to mention Jon Snow getting it on with his auntie. In fact, come to think of it, it seems that coitus with your kin is as much a part of *Game of Thrones* as dragons, drunkenness and death.

So, in celebration (or commiseration) of a gene pool that's shallower than some of Season 8's story arcs, why not tickle your taste buds with this aptly named tipple?

RECIPE

INGREDIENTS

1 oz white rum
1 oz Cointreau
1 oz cognac
1/2 oz lemon juice
Sugar
Ice

*"The things
I do for love."*
—JAIME LANNISTER

METHOD

1 Combine the white rum, Cointreau, lemon juice and cognac in a cocktail shaker with ice.

2 Shake thoroughly.

3 Rim the cocktail glass with sugar and pour in.

OLD (NAN) FASHIONED

SHE'S ONE of the oldest things in Winterfell, especially now that the crypts have been emptied of decomposing bodies. In fact, she's so old that she can remember a time when Hodor could say more than just "Hodor". We are, of course, talking about Old Nan, a toothless treasure with an encyclopaedic knowledge of terrifying tales from the Age of the First Men.

The Last Hero, The Ice Dragon, The Rat Cook: Old Nan's repertoire is full of classics. And when it comes to drinks, there's nothing more classic than the humble Old Fashioned, the granddaddy (or should that be Old Nanny) of cocktails. So what better way to pay homage to the old hag than with a libation that, like one of Nan's stories, we'll never get tired of.

"I know a story about a boy who hated stories."
—OLD NAN

RECIPE

INGREDIENTS

2 oz bourbon
2 dashes Angostura
  bitters
1 sugar cube
Orange twist, to garnish

METHOD

1 Place your sugar cube in an Old Fashioned glass, then wet it with the bitters and a small splash of water.

2 Crush the sugar cube with a bar spoon, pour in the whiskey, and add a single large ice cube.

3 Stir thoroughly. Then when you think you're done, stir again – you're aiming for about the length of one of Old Nan's stories here.

4 Twist your orange peel over the rim of the glass to release the oils, then drop in the drink before serving.

ROBIN ARRYN'S MILKSHAKE

GAME OF THRONES has treated us to all manner of horrors during the TV show's eight-season run. We've seen heroes beheaded, cities sacked and innocents tortured. There is no doubt, however, that the most creepy visual came not from blood or gore, but from Lysa Arryn's mothering of her "Sweetrobin" – a particularly yucky display of parenting that saw her son continue to treat her like a milk carton well into his early teens.

While Lisa Arryn's milkshake may bring all the boys to the Vale, rest assured that our creamy cocktail has everything you need to help your guests grow up big and strong.

RECIPE

INGREDIENTS

- 1 scoop vanilla ice cream
- 1 scoop chocolate ice cream
- 1 tablespoon chocolate sauce
- 2 cups Lysa Arryn's breastmilk (whole milk will do if you can't get a hold of the real thing)
- 2 oz Irish cream liqueur
- Cocoa powder / Whipped cream / Sprinkles / Chocolate shavings, to garnish

METHOD

1 Mix all of the liquid ingredients, along with the ice cream, in a blender and blitz until smooth.

2 Pour the milkshake mixture into a glass rimmed with cocoa powder. Top with whipped cream, sprinkles, chocolate shavings and any other garnishes that tickle your fancy.

3 Throw it down your mouth hole with all of the relish of Petyr Baelish flinging his wife out of the Moon Door.

"Mummy, I want to see the bad man fly."
—ROBIN ARRYN, LORD OF THE VALE

NEDNOG

IT SEEMS like a lifetime ago now that Sean Bean was serving as the honourable heart of *Game of Thrones*. His character, Ned Stark, was the moral compass of the entire saga, a weathervane of what is right and wrong, or black and white, in a story that seemed obsessed with delving into the various shades of grey that lie between the two.

He also had his head separated from his shoulders during the show's first season, laying the foundations for the shock and awe of the unceremoniously slaughtered characters that became *Game of Thrones'* calling card. Even now, after thousands of pages of prose and hundreds of hours of episodic entertainment have passed, Ned's shadow still looms large over the Seven Kingdoms.

As a result, we simply couldn't omit the Warden of the North and the true Lord of Winterfell from our own *Gin of Thrones*. And what better way to celebrate Lord Eddard Stark than a drink that is as white as the snows of the North and as sweet as its residents?

"The man who mixes the ingredients should drink the cocktail."
—EDDARD STARK

RECIPE

INGREDIENTS

4 oz spiced rum
8 oz bourbon
6 eggs, separated
3/4 cup sugar
32 oz whole milk
16 oz heavy cream
1 whole nutmeg

**WARNING* This
drink contains raw eggs,
not to mention alcohol,
which means that, if
you're pregnant or elderly,
it could be as bad for your
health as a Stark's visit to
King's Landing.*

METHOD

1 In a large mixing bowl, combine the egg yolks with half a cup of sugar and beat violently, like Ned punishing a Night's Watch deserter.

2 Stir in the milk, heavy cream, bourbon and rum.

3 In a separate bowl, whisk together the egg whites and remaining sugar until they form peaks as stiff and white as the battlements of Winterfell in winter.

4 Fold about a third of the mixture (more if desired) into the other bowl.

5 Serve in teacups with a topping of freshly grated nutmeg.

DOTHRAKI FERMENTED MARE'S MILK

THE DESERT of the Dothraki Sea can be a thirsty place. For those looking to scratch their alcoholic itch while in its vast expanse, a flagon of Fermented Mare's Milk will almost certainly be the tipple of choice.

The preferred poison of the hair-braided, heart-eating horse lords of Essos, Fermented Mare's Milk has been described as "half-clotted and heavy" by some fair-haired philistines. However, they clearly haven't tried our modern take on this Dothraki delicacy, a contemporary concoction that's designed to tickle the taste buds of an altogether more discerning class of imbiber – like yourself.

RECIPE

INGREDIENTS

1 oz cognac
1/2 oz rum
2 oz milk
1 oz cream
1/2 oz vanilla syrup
Cinnamon stick and
   nutmeg, to garnish

METHOD

1 Find a mare and milk it.

2 If you don't have a mare to hand, add all of the ingredients into a cocktail shaker filled with ice.

3 Shake the mixture vigorously.

4 Strain into a highball glass and garnish with grated nutmeg and a cinnamon stick.

"Yer jalan atthirari anni. (You are the drink of my life.)"
—KHAL DROGO

BAR SNACK: DEVILLED (DRAGON) EGGS

LET'S BE honest, we've all watched *Game of Thrones* and thought how awesome it would be to have dragons of our own. Just imagine it: you could fly them high above the Seven Kingdoms, barbecue your enemies and definitely give them better names (who came up with Drogon anyway? It's like calling your dog "dag").

But while we can't help you to lay your hands on the real thing, we have come up with a delicious dish that's worthy of Daenerys herself.

"Dragon's eggs, from the Shadow Lands beyond Asshai. The eons have turned them to stone, yet still they burn bright with beauty."

—MAGISTER ILLYRIO MOPATIS

RECIPE

INGREDIENTS

12 eggs (normal ones
will do you if you
can't find the dragon
variety)
1/4 cup mayonnaise
2 teaspoons Dijon
mustard
Pinch of salt
Pinch of pepper
Paprika and chopped
chives, to garnish

METHOD

1 Hard boil your eggs in a pan –
there's no need to carry them into
your dead husband's funeral pyre
(unless you want to).

2 Peel the eggs and cut in half
lengthways.

3 Scoop out the yolks with a teaspoon
and place in a bowl, setting the
whites aside for later.

4 Mix the yolks, mustard and
seasoning together.

5 Spoon the yolk mixture back
into the egg whites and sprinkle
with paprika before topping with
chopped chives.

SEASON 1 DRINKING GAME

GUARANTEED TO down you faster than George R. R. Martin's pen, our *Game of Thrones* Season 1 drinking game is not for the faint of heart. Indeed, this is perfect for those looking to relive the show's debut season – a simpler time when Sean Bean was still alive and the thought of Joffrey ascending to the Iron Throne was the stuff of nightmares.

So gather your Khalasar and get ready to drink your way through Westeros. Just remember, whatever you do, to please drink responsibly and leave the blind staggering to the White Walkers.

"When you play the Game of Thrones drinking game you win, or you die. There is no middle ground."

—CERSEI LANNISTER

RULES

 If a character drinks on screen, you drink.

 Take a sip every time
- someone calls Jon Snow a "bastard".
- Sean Bean does something honourable.
- anyone mentions "winter".
- you see gratuitous nudity in the background of an otherwise normal scene.
- Robert Baratheon swears.

Finish your drink if
- a character says "A Lannister always pays their debts".
- Cersei is mean to someone.
- a raven delivers a message.
- a king, or someone who thinks he should be king, dies.

Drink for the duration when
- there is a direwolf on screen.
- there's a sex scene.
  When they, ahem, finish, you finish.

 Down a shot every time
- someone is killed.
- Varys's manhood, or lack thereof, is discussed.
- Khal Drogo glares menacingly.*

---

* Depending on your definition of a glare, this one could floor you quicker than a Dothraki wedding.

SEASON

2

MAI TYWIN (LANNISTER)

A TIKI-THEMED cocktail might seem like it is a little too much fun for a character whose demeanour was colder than an Iron Banker's heart during his time in Westeros. But given that *Mai Tai* is Tahitian for "the best", we had no other choice but to name this tipple in Tywin Lannister's honour.

After all, in both the HBO adaptation and the books on which it is based, Tywin is a man that we all loved to hate – a deliciously macabre villain who was cold, calculating and eminently quotable. Like the emblematic animal emblazoned across the sigil of his House, Tywin was a symbol of strength, and the guiding hand behind many of the political machinations of the show up until his extremely timely demise. Yes, there was plenty of evil in his ledger, but anyone who lets their horse poop in the throne room and mockingly sends King Joffrey to bed in front of his advisors is worthy of celebration in our book.

RECIPE

INGREDIENTS

1 1/2 oz white rum
1/2 oz dark rum
3/4 oz orange curaçao
3/4 oz fresh lime juice
1/2 oz orgeat syrup
(almond extract or
simple syrup are good
alternatives if you
cannot get your hands
on the real thing)
Dash of grenadine
Lime wheel / Mint
sprig, to garnish

METHOD

1 Combine all of the ingredients
(except the dark rum) alongside
a mint sprig with ice in a cocktail
shaker.

2 Mix thoroughly.

3 Strain the mixture into an Old
Fashioned glass.

4 Float the dark rum over the top of
the drink using the back of a spoon.

5 Garnish with a lime wheel and mint
sprig.

*"You can drink. You can
joke. You can engage
in juvenile attempts
to make your father
uncomfortable."*
—TYWIN LANNISTER

IRON ISLANDS
ICED TEA

THE GREYJOYS aren't exactly the most fashionable House when it comes to picking your allegiance in *Game of Thrones*. The Lannisters have gold, the Starks have honour and the Targaryen's have dragons; the Greyjoys, however, are little more than a family of pirates obsessed with pillaging the Seven Kingdoms and picking fights with anyone and everyone who stands in their way.

"What is drunk may never die!"
—IRON ISLANDS, ANON

But from Theon and Yara to the under-appreciated Euron (who is sadly reduced to a poor man's Captain Jack Sparrow in the HBO series) the Iron Islands is home to some of George R. R. Martin's most engaging creations. So get ready to praise the Drowned God with a hot mess of a cocktail that's so boozy it will leave you stumbling like an Iron Fleet sailor on shore leave.

INGREDIENTS

¾ oz vodka
¾ oz white rum
¾ oz tequila
¾ oz gin
¾ oz triple sec
¾ oz simple syrup
¾ oz lemon juice
Cola, to taste
Lemon wedge, to
  garnish

METHOD

1 Add all of the ingredients, except the cola, into a highball glass with ice and stir.

2 Top with a splash of cola.

3 Garnish with a lemon wedge and a straw.

SHADE OF THE EVENING

Hands up – who remembers way back in Season 2 when some shaven-headed Warlocks stole Daenerys's dragons? Looking back now, the sequence was more important than we realized – a hefty piece of foreshadowing of the events that took place during the show's final season.

More importantly, it also introduced us to one of Westeros's most colourful concoctions, Shade of the Evening. A particular favourite with the Warlocks of the House of the Undying, this drink is a Qarth delicacy that's said to turn your lips blue and your mind soft. We're not promising that our own take on this Essos libation will do the same, but it certainly does look pretty in a glass!

"It turns their lips blue, and their minds soft."
—Xaro Xhoan Daxos

RECIPE

INGREDIENTS

1 1/2 oz vodka
1 1/2 oz blue curaçao
4 oz lemonade
Splash of freshly
   squeezed lime juice
Lemon wheel and
   cocktail cherry, to
   garnish

METHOD

1 Add the vodka, lemonade and lime juice to a cocktail shaker filled with ice and mix thoroughly.

2 Strain the mixture into a highball glass filled with ice.

3 Drizzle the blue curaçao over the top.

4 Give it a tropical top-off with a lemon wheel and cocktail cherry.

MARGARITA TYRELL

NEED A drink? Imagine how poor Margaery Tyrell must have felt. The eligible bachelorette of Highgarden was engaged to not one, not two, but three different men with claims to the Iron Throne during her eventful stint in Westeros. And all of them met grizzly ends.

First was poor Renly Baratheon, more interested in her brother than he was his bride to be. Then came Joffrey, a megalomaniacal pubescent with a penchant for crossbows who met his maker on their wedding day. Finally, there was sweet King Tommen, who killed himself after Margaery was blown up – along with the rest of her family – when Cersei set off a batch of wildfire in the Great Sept of Baelor.

I don't know about you, but just reading that is enough to make us want a stiff drink! So here we go...

RECIPE

INGREDIENTS

2 oz tequila
1 oz fresh lime juice
1/2 oz triple sec
1/2 oz agave syrup
Lime wedge / Salt, to
garnish

METHOD

1 Chill a margarita glass.

2 Pour all of your ingredients into a
cocktail shaker filled with ice and
mix thoroughly.

3 Take a lime wedge and run it
around the edge of your glass
before rolling the rim in salt.

4 Strain your cocktail mix into the
glass and garnish with a wedge of
lime.

*"The duty of any
wife, to any husband.
To provide him with
drink."*
—MARGAERY TYRELL

WILDFIRE

Before the Order of the Maesters, the Seven Kingdoms turned to the Alchemists for guidance. Famed for their love of fire, the people's pyromaniacs had seen their power wane since the reign of the Mad King, or at least that was until Tyrion Lannister employed their abilities in the Battle of the Blackwater.

The Alchemists are the only people in Westeros with the knowledge to produce wildfire, a rare concoction that burns bright green, melting flesh, steel and stone as easily as if it were kindling. Without it, *Game of Thrones* would have been over before it had even begun, and the Sept of Baelor might not have been destroyed (at least until Daenerys Targaryen's Season 8 strop, that is).

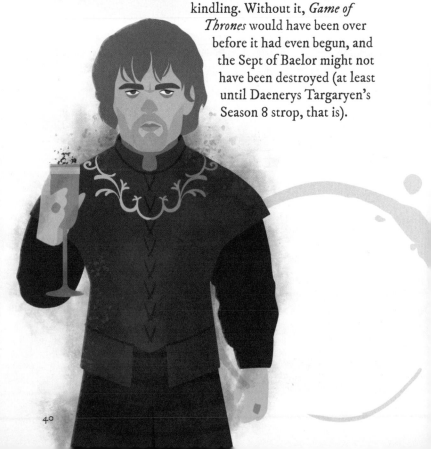

"The substance flows through my veins, and lives in the heart of every pyromancer. We respect its power."
—HALLYNE THE PYROMANCER

INGREDIENTS

1/2 oz blue curaçao
1/2 oz crème de menthe
1 teaspoon 151 proof
   rum

METHOD

1 Pour the crème de menthe into a
  shot glass.

2 Add the blue curaçao.

3 Top with 151 proof rum, and ignite
  using a match or lighter.

WARNING
*Remember to extinguish
before consuming, unless
you want to become the
latest offering to the Lord
of Light.*

BAR SNACK: ~~STALLION~~ ARTICHOKE HEARTS

W HILE THE Dothraki believe that it's a tasty treat – one that you'd feed to a pregnant lady no less – we're pretty sure that a raw stallion's heart isn't the kind of dish that you, dear reader, would happily order from a restaurant menu. That's why we've cooked up an alternative recipe for the equine appetizer – one with altogether less blood than the organ Daenerys chowed down on during a special ceremony at Vaes Dothrak.

Sure, it might not guarantee that your unborn prince grows up strong, swift and fearless, but swapping out a stallion's internal organs for the humble artichoke is tastier. It's also far less likely to leave you in need of the old rainbow yawn too.

"Khalakka dothrae mr'anha! (A prince rides within me!)"
—DAENERYS TARGARYEN

RECIPE

INGREDIENTS

1 cup breadcrumbs
1/2 cup parmesan cheese
1/2 cup salted butter
15 oz canned artichoke
   hearts
Parsley

METHOD

1 Preheat your oven to 390°F
   (200°C) and line a baking sheet
   with parchment paper.

2 While the oven is warming, drain
   and rinse your tinned artichoke
   hearts then pat dry with a kitchen
   towel.

3 Melt your butter in a saucepan until
   it resembles molten gold – do not
   tip it over your head to form an
   impromptu crown, however.

4 Combine breadcrumbs and
   parmesan in a bowl and season
   generously.

5 Dip your artichoke hearts in the
   molten butter, then roll them in
   your breadcrumb mix.

6 Bake for 15 minutes,
   then flip and bake for 15
   minutes more, or until
   the outside is as golden
   as the sands of the
   Dothraki desert.

SEASON 2 DRINKING GAME

Things were so much happier back in Season 2 of the show: Robb Stark, and his impossibly chiselled cheekbones, was still the King in the North; Jon Snow knew nothing; Daenerys was just an innocent young widow with three baby dragons to her name; and the Night King was still just one of Old Nan's bedtime stories.

They were simpler times. But if you're looking to complicate matters, why not try our Season 2 drinking game? It's the perfect excuse to imbibe copious amounts of alcohol while reminiscing about your favourite fictional characters.

Get ready to drink until you know nothing.

RULES

 If a character drinks on screen, you drink.

 Take a sip every time
- someone yells "King in the North".
- someone says Valor Morghulis.
- Hodor says "Hodor".
- a sword is drawn.

 Finish your drink if
- someone claims the Iron Throne is rightfully theirs.
- Daenerys calls herself the Mother of Dragons.
- Sam does something cowardly.

 Drink for the duration when
- there's incest!
- Ygritte tells Jon Snow he knows nothing.

Down a shot every time
- a major character dies.
- Arya vows to kill someone.
- Melisandre burns something.
- someone calls Arya "Boy".

SEASON

3

SHAKEN NOT LANNISTIRRED

A FAMILY BLESSED with limitless riches, a shallow gene pool and cheekbones so sharp they cut like Valyrian steel, the Lannisters are to *Game of Thrones* what the Ewings were to *Dallas* and the Sopranos were to, er, *The Sopranos*.

Whether it's Cersei's sneer, Tyrion's wit, Jaime's king slaying or Tywin's sinister plotting, the family that always pays its debts has had a (golden) hand in just about every major event that's shaken the Seven Kingdoms. So, in celebration of the lion-sigilled-sibling fanciers, and Jaime's unfortunate amputation, we put together this unique take on the classic martini to create a delicious drink that's guaranteed to quench your thirst for power.

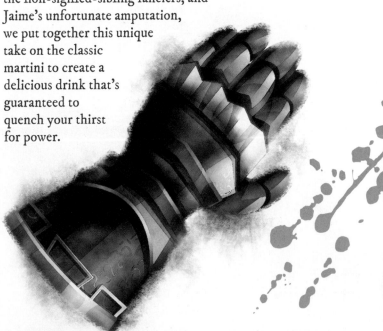

RECIPE

INGREDIENTS

1 oz good quality vodka
1 oz Goldschläger
   cinnamon schnapps
   (a liqueur with gold
   flakes – this is a
   Lannister cocktail
   after all)
Lemon twist, to garnish

METHOD

1 Fill a cocktail shaker with ice.

2 Add your alcohol and shake
   vigorously.

3 Strain the mixture into a chilled
   cocktail glass.

4 Twist your lemon over the mixture
   and drop the rind into the top of
   your glass.

*"Drinking and lust.
No man can match me
in these things. I am the
god of tits and wine."*
—TYRION LANNISTER

YOU KNOW NOTHING, JON SNOW(BALL)

WHETHER HE's hunting wildlings beyond the Wall, uniting the armies of men against the Night King or offering "advice" to his auntie, Jon Snow is *Game of Thrones*' perennial do-gooder. If the show was real life – and let's take a moment to be thankful that it's not – he would almost certainly be your designated driver on a night out: an honourable, stoic individual who's less likely to crack a smile than Cersei Lannister at a children's birthday party.

But all work and no play makes Jon a dull boy, which is why we've concocted a cocktail in his honour. Easier on the eyes than Kit Harrington and as sharp on your tongue as Ygritte's infamous put-downs, this drink will put a smile on your face quicker than you can say Aegon Targaryen.

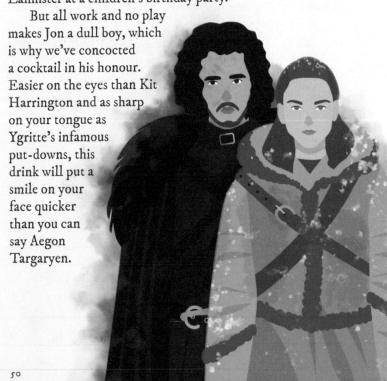

RECIPE

INGREDIENTS

2 oz advocaat
2 oz sparkling lemonade
Ice, to serve
1 maraschino cherry
   and lemon wedge, to
   garnish

METHOD

1 Mix the advocaat and lemonade in a
   tall glass filled with ice.

2 Stir until the outside of the glass
   feels as cold as a Castle Black
   outhouse.

3 Garnish with the maraschino cherry
   and lemon wedge, and enjoy.

*"Vomiting is not
celebrating."*
—JON SNOW

THOROS OF MYRMOSA

THE DRUNKEST man that Westeros ever saw, Thoros of Myr was a priest turned warrior who fought with King Robert Baratheon at the Siege of Pike – a battle he would later admit to not even remember on account of his inebriation. Thoros plays a prominent role in the Brotherhood Without Banners, even going beyond the Wall during Season 7. Perhaps he is best known for bringing Lord Beric Dondarrion back from dead, reviving the one-eyed warrior in much the same way that the classic mimosa can cure even the harshest of hangovers. In celebration of Thoros, why not whip up a batch of this classic cocktail – a breakfast drink that will light up your morning like a flaming sword.

RECIPE

INGREDIENTS

1 part sparkling wine
1 part freshly squeezed
  orange juice
Orange wedge, to
  garnish
For an extra kick, add
  a shot of vodka or
  Grand Marnier.

METHOD

1 Mix the orange juice and sparkling
  wine in a champagne flute.

2 Garnish with the orange wedge and
  drink until the Lord of Light sends
  you visions in the flames.

*"There's no story so good a drink
won't make it better."*
—THOROS OF MYR

HOT (PIE) TODDY

WHILE THE rest of Westeros was seemingly intent on staking a claim to the Iron Throne (or killing those who did), Hot Pie had a far simpler calling. He was no knight, wizard, warlock or wise man. Instead, Hot Pie was a master of the baked arts, as adept with a rolling pin as Jaime Lannister was with Valyrian steel.

The character was played impeccably by Ben Hawkey, who has gone on to prove that life imitates art by opening his own bakery. As for Hot Pie himself? Well, he was last seen at the Inn at the Crossroads, and although we don't know what fate befell the broad-stomached baker's boy, we like to think that this loveable foodie is seeing out the peace in Westeros in a pastry-filled paradise of his own making. Who knows, perhaps he's even enjoying the occasional cocktail named in his honour!

"Oh, and the gravy! Don't get me started on the gravy. Very difficult to get right. See, a lot of people give up on the gravy. You cannot give up on the gravy."
—HOT PIE

RECIPE

INGREDIENTS

1 oz bourbon (scotch or brandy make excellent alternatives)
1 tablespoon mild honey
2 teaspoons fresh lemon juice
1/4 cup hot water
Lemon slice and cinnamon stick, to garnish

METHOD

1 Put the bourbon, honey and lemon juice in a mug.

2 Top the mixture up with hot water and stir until everything is dissolved.

3 Garnish with a lemon slice and cinnamon stick.

THE LITTLE LION

THANKS TO their obscene amounts of wealth, the Lannisters are Westerosi celebrities. Think of them like the Seven Kingdoms' equivalent of the Kardashians, only without the Instagram accounts and reality-TV shows. Fair-haired, fresh-faced and filthy rich (and often just filthy), they are among the greatest Houses in all of Westeros. Or at least they were until Cersei, Jaime, Tywin and Lancel (remember him?) all met their makers while attempting to cling to power in King's Landing.

But the House lives on, largely thanks to the ludicrous amount of gold buried beneath Casterly Rock. So, in celebration of the House that is now helmed by the Little Lion himself, here's a tasty little shot that pays homage to the font of wealth ensuring the Lannister's have – and always will – pay their debts.

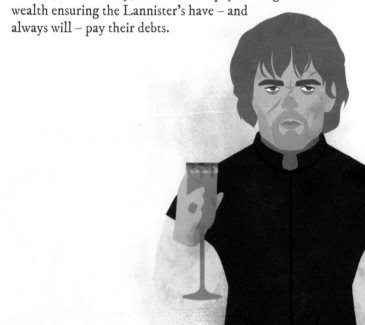

RECIPE

INGREDIENTS

3/4 oz Goldschläger
   cinnamon schnapps
3/4 oz spiced rum

METHOD

1 Pour the Goldschläger into a chilled shot glass.

2 Float the spiced rum on top by pouring it slowly over the back of a spoon to create two separate layers.

"It's not easy being drunk all the time. Everyone would do it if it were easy."
—Tyrion Lannister

THE BLOODY MARRY (AKA THE RED WEDDING!)

GAME OF THRONES' wealth of success has in part been built upon its ability to rope-a-dope its fans at every turn. But even for a story that boasts more shocks than a tradeshow for Taser manufacturers, the blood-curdling events of the Red Wedding stand out as something special.

One of the most disturbing moments to ever grace our TV screens, the cut-and-thrust of the Red Wedding set a high watermark against which the show has been measured ever since. It's also the inspiration behind our Bloody Marry, a drink which, like the infamous festivities from which it takes its name, packs the kind of punch that will leave you and your drinking chums groggily humming the "Rains of Castamere" in stunned disbelief for days afterward.

"The Lannisters send their regards."
—ROOSE BOLTON

RECIPE

INGREDIENTS

2 oz vodka
Tomato juice
1 tablespoon lemon juice
Worcestershire sauce
Tabasco sauce
Celery salt
Black pepper
Celery sticks, olives
   and lemon slices, to
   garnish
Ice

METHOD

1 Place the ice in a large glass and add the vodka and the lemon juice.

2 Top with tomato juice until the glass is almost full.

3 Add three dashes of Worcestershire and Tabasco sauce (or more if you want to make things as spicy as Robb Stark's relationship with Talisa), as well as a pinch of celery salt and black pepper.

4 Stir well.

5 Spear the olives on a cocktail stick, and add lemon slices and celery sticks to garnish.

BAR SNACK: THEON'S COCKTAIL WEENIES

I<small>T'S ONE</small> of the most disturbing moments in *Game of Thrones'* entire run, which is saying something for a show that's served up a smorgasbord of torture, assault and psychological damage during the course of its eight-season run. But nevertheless, the moment when Ramsay Bolton tortures Theon Greyjoy, castrates him and then waggles a sausage in his face for good measure still sticks long in the memory.

Granted, it's not the most appetizing of encounters. But it is iconic and, for that reason, Theon's favourite toy deserves to be honoured in porky posterity at your next Seven Kingdoms-themed soiree.

RECIPE

INGREDIENTS

1 pack of cocktail
  wieners (if you're
  interested in a
  bigger sausage, say
  something Podrick-
  sized, then opt for
  bratwurst instead)
1 bottle of your
  favourite BBQ sauce
Cocktail sticks, to serve

METHOD

1 Combine the sausages and BBQ
  sauce in a pan and cook for 10
  minutes (longer if bratwurst is
  used), or until sticky.

2 Allow to cool, then place the
  sausages on cocktail sticks to serve
  – just make sure to stick them with
  the pointy end.

"This is turning into a lovely evening."
—RAMSAY BOLTON

SEASON 3 DRINKING GAME

WILDER THAN a night at Craster's Keep and with more victims than your average Red Wedding, what better way is there to binge watch the third (and some would say best) season of your favourite show than with a bit of binge drinking?

So grab your (dragon)glass and get ready to drink like an imp on his wedding night. Just remember that if you start to stare into the middle distance like a Three-Eyed Raven or out-douche King Joffrey, it's probably time to take a break.

*Best enjoyed with friends (if, unlike Joffrey, you have any), make sure you assign each of your drinking party a House (Barratheon, Stark, Lannister, Greyjoy, Tyrell and Targaryen are this season's most common). Trust us, it's more fun this way.

"If you think this has a happy ending, you haven't been paying attention."
—RAMSAY BOLTON

RULES

 If the House you have been assigned is mentioned, drink!

 Take a sip every time
- Joffrey whines about something. (Yes, that's whines, not wines. Stay focused, people!)
- someone questions Jon Snow's allegiance.
- someone mentions religion.

 Finish your drink if
- you see someone's bare behind on screen. There's a lot of moonshine in this season.
- someone describes one of the Frey daughters as ugly.
- someone calls Jaime "Kingslayer".

Drink for the duration when

- Tyrion drinks on screen. Be warned: this is by far his booziest season to date.
- Theon is being tortured. It might not numb his pain, but it will certainly ease yours.

Down a shot every time

- someone has a body part severed.
- Daenerys speaks a foreign language.
- Bran's voice breaks mid-line – it turns out even Three-Eyed Ravens aren't immune to the ravages of puberty.

SEASON

4

MILK OF THE POPPY

WESTEROS ISN'T the most progressive of realms when it comes to the medical sciences. Catch greyscale and the chances are that you'll be left to turn into a stone monster. Lose a limb and, unless you're rich enough to afford a solid-gold prosthetic, you'll have to learn to live with it. Get stabbed by a poisoned spear, and you're more likely to come back as some kind of malformed zombie than make a full recovery. You get the idea. What we're really trying to say is that Westeros isn't the kind of place you want to travel to without insurance.

But despite their deficiencies, when it comes to medicine the Westerosi have got at least one thing right, and that's pain-killing. From headaches to spear wounds, via severed limbs, surgical procedures and probably even the common cold, Milk of the Poppy seems to be the catch-all cure for what ails the Seven Kingdoms.

We're obviously not going to recommend you start taking opium, so instead we've crafted a libation that will numb your pain and put a smile on your face in the process.

"Maester, could I trouble you for some milk of the poppy? A thimble cup will suffice."
—DORAN MARTELL

RECIPE

INGREDIENTS

1 ¾ oz Bénédictine
herbal liqueur
Milk
Cinnamon stick, to
garnish

METHOD

1 Fill a mug with ice.

2 Add the Bénédictine and top
with cold milk (or forget the ice
and add hot milk for a warming
alternative).

3 Garnish with a cinnamon stick.

MOTHER OF DRAGON (FRUIT)

For a while, Daenerys Targaryen was the best thing to happen to *Game of Thrones*. Inspirational leader, Mother of Dragons, badass Breaker of Chains, she was kicking slaver arse and getting stuff done over on Essos – all the while threatening to break the wheel across the Narrow Sea in Westeros too. Dany was so popular that the show's best characters were flocking to her cause. And fans? Well, they were so Team Targaryen that they even started to name their children after her.

But then, sometime around the beginning of Season 8, things began to turn sourer than a flagon of fermented mare's milk for our white-haired queen. There was that unfortunate business of sleeping with her nephew, not to mention the rising tensions with Sansa and anyone else who wouldn't immediately "bend the knee". Then, finally, Daenerys turned full heel, barbecuing the unfortunate residents of King's Landing and transforming into an evil tyrant in the process.

Still, we'll always have Astapor and, to celebrate happier times, here's a drink so refreshing it could quench even the Mother of Dragons' thirst for power.

"I will do what queens do. I will drink."

—Daenerys Targaryen

RECIPE

INGREDIENTS

1 1/2 oz white rum
1/2 oz simple syrup
3 oz soda water
1 lime, cut into wedges
1 dragon fruit
6 mint leaves

METHOD

1 Chop the top off of your dragon fruit and scoop out the flesh from the inside.

2 Place the dragon fruit, mint leaves, lime wedges and simple syrup into a highball glass and muddle.

3 Add the rum and top with soda water as desired.

4 Garnish with lime wedges, strips of dragon fruit skin and fresh mint leaves.

TEQUILA SUNSPEAR

WHILE THE rest of Westeros is obsessed with honour, etiquette and the seemingly never-ending quest for the Iron Throne, the Dornish are a little different to say the least. A land of liberal lovers whose penchant for the kind of entertainment you'll find at Little Finger's establishments knows no bounds, they're also a particularly fiery bunch. This was displayed emphatically by fan favourite Oberyn Martell, the smooth-talking, spear-wielding Red Viper who showed us that showboating has no place in trial by combat.

If you're looking for an eye-popping cocktail to take the sour taste of Oberyn's death out of your mouth, have a bang on the Tequila Sunspear – a Dornish-inspired concoction that's as sexy as a pit of Sand Snakes, as sassy as Oberyn's sartorial choices and packs the same kind of punch as one of his poison-dipped spears to boot.

"The Targaryens talk of fire and blood. In Dorne, our blood is fire."
—PRINCE OBERYN MARTELL

RECIPE

INGREDIENTS

2 oz tequila
3 oz orange juice
  (freshly squeezed
  seems appropriate
  given the nature of
  Oberyn's unfortunate
  demise)
1 teaspoon grenadine
Ice
Cherry and orange
  slice, to garnish

METHOD

1 Combine the tequila, orange juice
  and ice in a cocktail shaker and mix
  well.

2 Strain into a chilled highball glass.

3 Slowly pour the grenadine over
  the top, so that it creates a multi-
  layered effect.

4 Garnish with a cherry and orange
  slices.

HARVEY (THE) WALLBANGER

I T'S ONE of Westeros's most recognisable landmarks, a colossal structure stretching for 100 leagues across the realm's northern border. Standing at over 700 feet tall, the frozen fortification has been the backdrop against which many of *Game of Thrones'* most memorable moments have occurred. It's where Jon Snow spent much of his time, where epic battles took place and where the Night King eventually marched his army of undead south with the help of a zombie dragon. It's even the spot where Tyrion relieved himself all the way back in the show's third episode.

The shield that guards the realm, its shadow has loomed large over the events in the Seven Kingdoms ever since the show first burst its way onto our screens. And what more fitting way to celebrate the millennia-old fortress of frost and stone than with a tasty tipple that's as much of a fixture on bar menus as the Wall is on a map of Westeros.

RECIPE

INGREDIENTS

1 1/2 oz vodka
1/2 oz Galliano
3 oz freshly squeezed
   orange juice
Orange slice, to garnish

METHOD

1 Stir the vodka and orange juice with
  ice in a highball glass.

2 Float the Galliano over the top
  using the back of a spoon.

3 Garnish with an orange slice and
  serve.

*"I just want to stand
on top of the Wall
and piss off the edge
of the world."*
—TYRION LANNISTER

SOBERYN MARTELL

ALL MEN must die but that doesn't mean that all men must drink. Just because the characters in *Game of Thrones* drink like fish doesn't mean you have to. After all, they're too busy worrying about having their heads lopped off by a broadsword or being burned alive by dragon fire to be concerned about the state of their livers, but what's your excuse?

Every good host should have a virgin cocktail up their sleeves. Never fear: just because your guest has chosen to forego alcohol doesn't mean they have to forego the fun. That's why we've cooked up this alcohol-free fancy – a Dornish red that's got all of the excitement you'd expect from a drink associated with the Red Viper, only without the sting.

If your poison of choice is no poison at all, this cocktail will be right up your street.

RECIPE

INGREDIENTS

1 oz grenadine syrup
4 oz ginger ale
4 oz lemon-lime soda
   (like 7-Up or Sprite)
Maraschino cherry, to
   garnish

METHOD

1 Fill a highball glass with ice.

2 Add all of the ingredients and stir
   until mixed.

3 Garnish with a cherry and enjoy.

*"I drink the right amount
too often."*
—SANDOR "THE
HOUND" CLEGANE

BAR SNACK: BRIE(NNE) OF TART(H)

I DON'T know about you, but I'm a card-carrying member of the Brienne of Tarth fan club. I cheered when she defeated the Hound in hand-to-hand combat, I cried when she got knighted before the Battle of Winterfell and I sighed when she embarked on a one-night stand with Jaime Lannister instead of making beautiful big-boned babies with Tormund Giantsbane.

Even in a tale that's crammed full of a kaleidoscope of incredible characters, Brienne stands out from the crowd – and not just because she's about a foot taller than everyone else on the show! So, in her honour, here's a snack that's big, strong and sure to be a fan favourite.

"Don't you mock me!"
—BRIENNE OF TARTH

RECIPE

INGREDIENTS

12 oz pre-made ready-
  rolled puff pastry
3 red onions
6 oz brie
3 1/2 oz cranberry sauce
1 tablespoon Dijon
  mustard
2 tablespoons white
  wine vinegar
1 tablespoon olive oil

METHOD

1 Preheat oven to 390°F (200°C).
  While the oven is doing its thing,
  unroll your pre-made pastry onto
  a baking tray and trim to shape and
  bake as instructed on the packet.

2 While the pastry is baking, heat
  the oil in a large pan. Add the
  onions and cook until soft and
  caramelized.

3 Stir in the vinegar, mustard and
  season well. Then remove the pan
  from the heat.

4 The pastry should be
  puffed up bigger than
  Brienne's chest after Jaime
  Lannister knighted her by
  now, so remove it from the oven.

5 Spread your caramelized-onion
  mixture over the surface and add
  a few blobs of cranberry sauce,
  scattered like the Hound's wounds,
  for good measure.

6 Finally, top with brie and a drizzle
  of oil, then return it to the oven
  until everything is melted and
  gooey and ready to eat.

SEASON 4 DRINKING GAME

MANY WOULD argue that Season 4 saw *Game of Thrones* at the peak of its powers. After all, this was the run that followed the Red Wedding and the subsequent explosion in popularity that it brought to the show. It's also jammed full of memorable moments. From Joffrey's wedding to Tyrion's trial, via Theon's torture, Ygritte's last words and the small matter of the face-off between fan favourites Gregor Clegane and Oberyn Martell.

So grab a flagon of your favourite Dornish red and get ready to toast King Joffrey – "Long may he reign" – with our ultimate Season 4 drinking game.

"Money buys a man's silence for a time. A drink buys it forever."
—PETYR BAELISH

RULES

 If Joffrey begins to choke, cheer loudly, then drink heavily.

 Take a sip every time
- Shae calls Tyrion her "Little Lion".
- we are reminded that Jon Snow knows nothing.
- Missandei utters any of Daenerys's titles when she introduces the Mother of Dragons, the Breaker of Chains, the Unburnt, Queen of the Andals, Khaleesi of the Great Grass Sea and so on and so forth.
- Oberyn Martell, AKA the Red Viper, taunts the Mountain during trial by combat.

Finish your drink if

- Arya reads off the names on her hit list.
- there is nudity on screen; this, after all, is Game of Thrones and, from boobs to bums, this season is like spending an evening in a brothel with Ser Bronn.
- someone calls Theon "Reek".

Drink for the duration when

- Bran wargs into someone or something. Bonus points if you yell "Hodor" while doing it.
- there's a character on screen that prompts you to ask, "What's their name again?" Then drink until you either remember what it is or you fall over, whichever comes first.

Down a shot every time
- a character dies. But be warned: this season is bloodier than a Lannister family feud with some truly crushing *wink wink* deaths.
- one of Daenerys's dragons appears on screen. Why not turn things all the way up to 11 by making it a shot of Fireball?

SEASON

5

THE NIGHT IS DARK 'N' STORMY AND FULL OF TERROR

Ah, Melisandre, the Red Priestess of R'hllor, the Lord of Light's most passionate cheerleader and a budding pyromaniac who'll set almost anything on fire if she thinks it will help her cause. She is one of *Game of Thrones'* most mysterious characters – a sultry siren who's just as good at bringing people back from the dead as she is at offing them with new-born shadow creatures.

Played superbly by Dutch actress Carice van Houten, the Red Woman deserves a cocktail that is as fiery and fierce as she is, a drink that will leave you breathless and burning but, above all, a drink with a really cool name!

"We all must choose. Man or woman, young or old, lord or peasant, our choices are the same. We choose sobriety or we choose drunkenness."

—Melisandre, the Red Woman

RECIPE

INGREDIENTS

2 oz dark rum

3 oz ginger beer (do not accidentally opt for ginger ale – you want this to burn like a little girl on a funeral pyre)

1/2 oz lime juice

Lime wedge, to garnish

METHOD

1 Fill a highball glass with ice cubes.

2 Add rum.

3 Top with ginger beer and lime juice, then stir until mixed.

4 Garnish with a lime wedge.

VALOR
MOR-GUINNESS

MYSTERIOUS, QUICK with a catchphrase and forever talking in riddles, Jaqen H'ghar is like the grizzled old boozehound who regularly props up the bar at your local watering hole. He's also one of the best characters to grace *Game of Thrones* and grants Arya three murder-wishes, a crash course in Braavosi and a mysterious coin after she rescues him from captivity.

A great character deserves a great drink, and what better way to celebrate a member of the House of Black and White than this Guinness-inspired cocktail. Just remember if you're not yelling, "All men must drink", as you knock back these delicious little thimbles of fun, then you're not doing it right!

"A minute, an hour, a month. Drunkenness is certain. The time is not."
—JAQEN H'GHAR

RECIPE

INGREDIENTS

2 oz coffee liqueur
1 oz Irish cream liqueur

METHOD

1 Fill a shot glass two-thirds full with coffee liqueur.

2 Top off the glass by pouring the Irish cream liqueur over the back of a spoon, so that it settles on top to form two layers.

BLOOD AND SAND (SNAKES)

Ask anyone who's read George R. R. Martin's books and they'll tell you that the HBO adaption criminally undersold the Sand Snakes, the badass bastards of Oberyn Martell. But despite their anaemic showing on the small screen, viewers did at least get to see the trio of deadly Dornish sirens spar with our favourite sellsword, Ser Bronn.

From their face-off in the Water Gardens to a prison scene that's hotter than a summer's day in Sunspear, it seemed like Blackwater's finest had truly met his match in Tyrene, Nymeria and Obara. To wash away the disappointment of their all too short stint on the series, here's a Westerosi-inspired take on a classic cocktail to help drown your Sand Snake-related sorrows.

"Go drink until you feel like you did the right thing."
—Ser Bronn of the Blackwater

RECIPE

INGREDIENTS

¾ oz scotch
¾ oz sweet vermouth
¾ oz cherry liqueur
¾ oz freshly squeezed
  orange juice
Orange peel, to garnish

METHOD

1 Mix all of the ingredients into a cocktail shaker with ice and shake vigorously.

2 Strain into a chilled cocktail glass.

3 Garnish with a twist of orange peel.

4 Enjoy smugly while you bore your guests with details about all the things the HBO show got wrong about the books.

BRRRRRRRRRRBON SOUR

You may not be a fully fledged member of the Night's Watch, but that doesn't mean you can't drink like you are. They're a hardy bunch, those Crows – a ragtag group of thieves and miscreants who are as cold and as hard as the weather on the Wall. In other words, they're exactly the kind of drinking buddies that will leave you with a raging hangover and a lifetime's supply of stories to tell.

So don your blackest furs and get ready to re-create a night in Castle Black with a cocktail so sour it will probably stab you through the heart for fraternising with the Free Folk.

"Hear my words and bear witness to my vow. Night gathers, and now my drinking begins."
—Oath of the Night's Watch

RECIPE

INGREDIENTS

1 1/2 oz bourbon
3/4 oz freshly squeezed
  lemon juice
1 tablespoon simple
  syrup
1 refrigerated egg white
Ice
Cherry, to garnish

METHOD

1 Pour all of the ingredients
  into a cocktail shaker and mix
  enthusiastically until it becomes
  white and frothy, like fresh
  snowfall on the Wall.

2 Add ice and shake again.

3 Strain into a glass and scoop any
  remaining froth from the cocktail
  shaker onto your drink with a
  spoon.

4 Garnish with one or two
  cherries on a cocktail stick sat
  atop the glass.

BAR SNACK: UNSULLIED SPICED NUTS

WE DON'T want to get too psychological on you, but the residents of *Game of Thrones* have a thing for lopping off each other's private parts. From Reek's torture to Varys's troubled childhood, Freud would have a field day with it.

By far the most famous eunuchs on the show, however, are the Unsullied: fierce warriors renowned for their discipline, skills in battle and the absence of certain appendages. Although that absence is slightly called into question after their visits to the brothels of Meereen in Season 5.

The product of centuries' worth of oppression from the Masters of Slaver's Bay, the soldiers are trained from the age of five, when they are castrated before being enrolled in a brutal training regime.

The thought of all that training makes us hungry, and what better way to sate your stomach than a handful of spiced nuts?

RECIPE

INGREDIENTS

3/4 cup sugar
1 tablespoon salt
1 tablespoon chilli
   powder
2 teaspoons cinnamon
2 teaspoons cayenne
   pepper
1 large egg white
4 cups raw nuts
   (cashews, almonds
   and pecans make a
   fine choice, or create
   your own mix)

METHOD

1 Preheat the oven to 300°F (150°C).

2 Coat a baking sheet in non-stick
   cooking spray.

3 In a small bowl, whisk the
   sugar, egg white, chilli powder,
   cinnamon, salt and cayenne until
   the mixture is frothy.

4 Add your nut mixture and toss.

5 Spread the coated nuts out on
   the baking sheet and cook for 45
   minutes.

6 Leave to cool, then enjoy.

"Lord Varys is right. I have been to Essos and seen the Unsullied first-hand. They are very impressive on the battlefield. Less so in the bedroom..."
—OBERYN MARTELL

SEASON 5 DRINKING GAME

Season 5 is to *Game of Thrones* as *The Empire Strikes Back* is to *Star Wars*. Everyone is on such a downer as the action unfolds in Westeros. Let's just look at the evidence *deep breath*: Jon is ruffling feathers with the crows in the Night's Watch; the Night King has shown up and swept all before him; Tyrion is depressed after offing his dad and the love of his life; Sansa is suffering at the hands of her new hubby; and Daenerys is struggling to keep order in Essos. Heck, even Cersei is having a rough ride of things.

Indeed, the only people who seem remotely happy during this ten-episode run are Ramsay Bolton, who's continuing his quest to become the Seven Kingdoms' most sinister bastard (pun intended), and King Tommen, who at the opposite end of the spectrum is head over heels in love with his Highgarden-born bae.

Don't worry, though: things might be depressing in the Seven Kingdoms, but we're here to raise your spirits with a drinking game that will put a bigger smile on your face than King Tommen after he's consummated his marriage. Ewwwwww.

"This is all I want to do. All day, every day, for the rest of my life."
—Tommen Baratheon

RULES

 If Tyrion drinks, you drink. Be warned: even for a time-honoured booze hound like Peter Dinklage's character, Season 5 is particularly alcoholic.

 Take a sip every time
- Arya gets smacked during her internship at the House of Black and White. Seriously, are there no child services in Braavos?
- someone says "Shame" during Cersei's Westerosi walk of shame.
- The Sand Snakes do something badass.

 Finish your drink if
- someone calls Jon Snow a "bastard".
- King Tommen looks doe-eyed at Margaery.

 Drink for the duration when
- a character is being barbecued on screen in honour of the Lord of Light. Twice as fast if you want to forget the fate of poor little Shireen Baratheon.

 Down a shot every time
- a character dies. But watch out because the Westerosi morgues are particularly busy this season. Maybe skip the more epic battle scenes – we don't want you to wind up in the hospital.
- The Night King is on screen.

SEASON

6

HODOR LIBRE

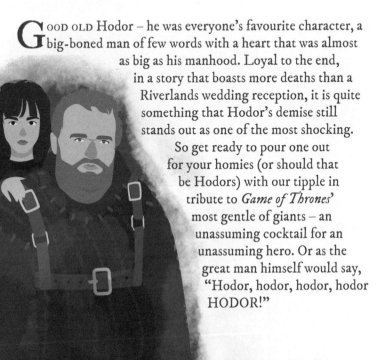

GOOD OLD Hodor – he was everyone's favourite character, a big-boned man of few words with a heart that was almost as big as his manhood. Loyal to the end, in a story that boasts more deaths than a Riverlands wedding reception, it is quite something that Hodor's demise still stands out as one of the most shocking. So get ready to pour one out for your homies (or should that be Hodors) with our tipple in tribute to *Game of Thrones'* most gentle of giants – an unassuming cocktail for an unassuming hero. Or as the great man himself would say, "Hodor, hodor, hodor, hodor HODOR!"

"Hold the door!"
—HODOR

RECIPE

INGREDIENTS

1 lime
2 oz dark rum
Cola to taste
Lime wedge, to garnish

METHOD

1 Squeeze your lime juice into a highball glass.

2 Add ice and rum and stir like HBO stirred your emotions in that fateful episode.

3 Top with cola, garnish with a lime wedge, and enjoy!

THE IMP'S DELIGHT

"**I**MP", "**M**ONSTER", "Half-man". Tyrion has been called all manner of names during his run on the show, but Peter Dinklage's character is, without a doubt, the biggest thing in Westeros. In a story that's filled with warriors, noble lords, powerful ladies and all manner of magical mischief makers, it says something that everyone's favourite character is a hard-drinking, straight-talking dwarf.

Not only does Tyrion enjoy one of the most engrossing arcs in the entire story, but he's also gifted with some of the best bits in both the books and the show. In celebration of *Game of Thrones'* poster boy of drinking and debauchery, we cooked up a cocktail to honour a vintage we all wish we could quaff.

RECIPE

INGREDIENTS

2 oz red wine
1 1/2 oz apple brandy
1/2 oz sloe gin
1/4 oz maple syrup
2 dashes Angostura
   bitters
Apple slice and freshly
   grated cinnamon, to
   garnish

METHOD

1 Combine all of the ingredients in a
   cocktail shaker filled with ice.

2 Stir the mixture like you're Tyrion
   hosting a meeting of the Small
   Council.

3 Strain into a chilled cocktail glass.

4 Garnish with a thin apple slice
   and a dusting of freshly grated
   cinnamon.

*"One day, after
our queen has taken
the Seven Kingdoms…
I'd like to have my
own vineyard. Make
my own wine – The
Imp's Delight. Only
my close friends could
drink it."*
—TYRION LANNISTER

TORMUND'S GINGER BEERD

Take one part giant and one part wildling, mix it together with a whole heap of hilarity, and you have everyone's favourite big-boned redhead. In a world where characters are liable to split fan opinion like a broadsword, the only constant is the world's mutual love for Tormund Giantsbane. Played on the show by Norwegian actor Kristofer Hivju, he's the closest thing to a hipster that the Free Folk have ever seen – minus a man bun and the small batch coffee shop in a disused industrial building, of course.

Wildling warrior, giant-milk lover and expert bear hugger, Tormund is many things. But he is, above all, a famed drinker whose ability to consume copious amounts of booze is only matched by his fearsomeness in battle. So if you're a fan of this flame-haired favourite, check out our recipe below for his Ginger Beerd.

RECIPE

INGREDIENTS

2 oz rye whiskey or
bourbon
6 oz good quality ginger
ale
Half a lemon
Mint and a lemon slice,
to garnish

METHOD

1 Fill a glass (or an animal horn if
you have one lying around) with
ice.

2 Pour in your alcohol of choice
alongside the juice of half a lemon.
Throw in the leftover zest and mix
well.

3 Top off with ginger ale, garnish
with a few mint leaves and a lemon
slice, and serve with a bawdy tale
and a rib-crushing hug.

*"I need a good drink
to help me sleep the
night before a fight.
You want some? I
have a jug of sour
goat's milk, stronger
than any of that grape
water you southern
twats like sucking on."*
—TORMUND
GIANTSBANE

GIN RICKON

THERE'S A good chance you don't remember Rickon Stark. After all, Ned's youngest son was one of the forgotten characters in *Game of Thrones*' TV adaptation. He was a boy with fewer lines than Hodor and a death scene during the Battle of the Bastards that had the internet up in arms about the best way to dodge an arrow – top tip: it's not run in a straight line over a vast, open battlefield.

In fact, while the rest of the Stark clan played a major part in the destiny of Westeros, poor Rickon was little more than an afterthought in the HBO show. The closest he came to being relevant was when Theon pretended to kill him. But to us, Rickon will always be much more than just another victim of Ramsay Bolton's own particular brand of brutality; he will be the boy that bantered with Osha, and not to mention the Stark who came up with the best direwolf name out of the entire family.

Although he may not have reached an age where he was allowed to drink it, we are sure he would have wanted you to enjoy this storied summertime sip – a classic refreshing treat that, like poor Rickon, is all too often forgotten about.

"Here, Shaggydog."
—RICKON STARK

RECIPE

INGREDIENTS

1 1/2 oz gin
1 lime
Club soda, to taste

METHOD

1 Fill a glass with ice.

2 Pour in your gin.

3 Chop your lime in half and juice it into the glass, then drop the emptied husks in for good measure.

4 Top with club soda and enjoy.

THE NARROW
SEA(BREEZE)

T HIS APTLY named body of water is all that separates
Westeros from Essos in the fictional world in which
Game of Thrones is set. It's not just a liquid landmark, however.
While the action regularly crossed its tides during the show's
run, the Narrow Sea also played an important role in shaping
many characters' lives. The Dothraki are scared of it, the Iron
Islanders worship it and Ser Davos has sailed on it for so long
that he knows it like the back of his hand (apart from the bits
he's missing, that is).

It also inspired our take on this classic concoction. A great-
tasting tipple that's brighter than a Highgarden flower show,
zingier than Bronn's best one-liners and smoother than Varys's
cranium.

RECIPE

INGREDIENTS

1 1/2 oz vodka
3 oz cranberry juice
1 oz grapefruit juice
Grapefruit slice, to
    garnish

METHOD

1 Pour the vodka and cranberry juice
  into a highball glass filled with ice.

2 Stir well.

3 Top with grapefruit juice and
  garnish.

*"Even a million
Dothraki are no
threat to the realm,
as long as they
remain on the other
side of the Narrow
Sea."*
—EDDARD STARK

BAR SNACK: SOUR CREAM AND ONION (KNIGHT) DIP

THE STARKS have direwolves, the Lannisters have the lion, and the Boltons have a flayed man (not the easiest thing to sew onto a banner, we imagine). Indeed, it seems that to succeed at life in the Seven Kingdoms you need a good sigil, something that will inspire honour in your men and terror in your enemies and perhaps something that is a key ingredient in a delicious dip?

Yes, you heard us right. While the rest of the Lords of Westeros were swinging their broadswords in a bid for glory, Ser Davos was quietly serving the realm under the most inauspicious of symbols. That's why we're paying tribute to one of Westeros's true heroes with a dip so delicious your guests will be desperate to smuggle the recipe away from you.

RECIPE

INGREDIENTS

1/3 cups oil (canola or grape seed work best)
1 medium onion
1/4 teaspoon sugar
1 cup sour cream
Pinch of salt

METHOD

1 Place a pan on the hob and add the oil.

2 While the pan is heating, finely chop your onion. Just be careful not to saw your fingers off, OK? Remember: we're making onion dip, not becoming an Onion Knight.

3 When the oil is hot, add your onions, salt and sugar and cook for around 10 minutes, or until the onion has browned.

4 Mix your onion mixture with sour cream and serve.

"Some highborn fools call you Onion Knight and think they insult you. So you take the onion for your sigil, sew it on your coat, fly the onion flag."
—STANNIS BARATHEON

SEASON 6 DRINKING GAME

Aꜰᴛᴇʀ ᴛʜᴇ unshakeable downer that was Season 5, this chapter of *Game of Thrones* is packed with high points, reunions and fist-pumping moments of awesomeness, all culminating in the Battle of the Bastards – after which Jon Snow was certain to have needed a very stiff drink. It's also one of the final points before the showrunners ran out of source material, forcing them to finish George R. R. Martin's work for him and annoy the entire internet in the process.

But we still have a way to go before you have to worry about that, so get ready to party like a newly anointed King of the North with our Season 6 drinking game.

"I drink because it feels good."
—Cᴇʀꜱᴇɪ Lᴀɴɴɪꜱᴛᴇʀ

RULES

 If Cersei drinks, you drink. Be warned, however, that her liver must be in worse shape than the Sept of Baelor if this season is anything to go by.

 Take a sip every time
- someone punches Ramsay Bolton in the face. Take two sips if you find it as satisfying as the rest of the world.
- somebody says "Hold the Door".
- there is a moment that makes you want to punch the air in delight. Finish your drink if it's the death of a particularly malevolent menace.

 Finish your drink if
- someone pledges allegiance to Daenerys.
- Arya kills someone – she's getting pretty good at it by now.

 Drink for the duration when
- Bran wargs into the past with the Three-Eyed Raven. Trust us, it makes the scenes go much faster.

 Down a shot every time
- Walder Frey makes you feel uncomfortable.
- Tyrion tells a dad joke.
- wannabe pyromaniac Daenerys destroys something with fire.

SEASON

7

JÄGERMAESTER

I N AMONGST the fighting, the conquests and the fire-breathing dragons, it's easy to forget that *Game of Thrones* isn't all about war and pillage. There's an incredibly rich world filled with carefully thought out factions and societal structures. Nowhere is this truer than with the Order of Maesters, a cabal of scientists, scholars and healers that have played a key role in the events in the Seven Kingdoms.

Whether it's the nobleness of Maester Aemon, the dark arts of Maester Qyburn, or the randy robe-clad figure of Maester Pycelle, both the TV show and the books on which it is based have given us a real glimpse into the chain-wearing order and their methods. Though it's probably likely to kill more brain cells than it creates, the Jägermaester is the perfect tipple for those looking forward to a night on the (Old)town.

RECIPE

INGREDIENTS

1 1/2 oz Jägermeister
Root beer
1 scoop vanilla ice
cream

METHOD

1 Pour your Jägermeister into a large
glass.

2 Top as desired with root beer.

3 Add a scoop of ice cream on top.

"The Citadel took my chain, but they could not take my drink."
—MAESTER QYBURN

SANSARAC

L OVER OF lemon cakes, Queen in the North, the perennially unlucky in love Sansa Stark has undergone more transformations during *Game of Thrones*' run than she has wardrobe changes. She has developed from a young girl who fawned over Joffrey, the Knight of Flowers and everything else about life in the Seven Kingdoms' capital, to a powerful leader with a keen mind for the politics of power. Like Sophie Turner – the actress who expertly plays her – Sansa has done a lot of growing up over the past decade in Westeros.

In honour of the Lady of Winterfell, here's a drink that's a stiff as the northern wind and with roots that go deeper than the castle's crypts. My lords and ladies, I give you the Sansarac.

"When the snows fall and the white winds blow, the lone wolf goes thirsty, but the pack imbibes."
—EDDARD STARK

RECIPE

INGREDIENTS

2 1/2 oz rye whiskey
1 sugar cube
2 dashes Peychaud's
  bitters
1 dash Angostura bitters
Absinthe
Lemon peel, to garnish

METHOD

1 In a cocktail shaker, muddle
  together a sugar cube with a few
  drops of water until they are mixed.

2 Add a handful of ice, the rye
  whiskey, bitters and combine well.

3 Place a dash of absinthe in an Old
  Fashioned glass and roll around
  until the surface is coated. Discard
  any excess.

4 Strain the contents of the cocktail
  shaker into your absinthe-coated
  glass, then garnish with a twist
  of lemon peel.

CERSEI'S SANGRIA

FEW DRINKERS in Westeros can ever hope to be quite as perennially pickled as Tyrion Lannister but, by the gods, that's not going to stop Cersei from trying. Judging by the amount of time she spends with a goblet in her hand, the Queen Regent is as familiar with the Red Keep's wine cellars as she is with the content of her brother's breeches.

But no woman, even Cersei, can exist on wine alone. That's why Maester Qyburn has spiced things up with this Seven Kingdoms' take on the classic Spanish sangria – a fruity concoction that provides the perfect way to unwind after a long day plotting your enemies' grizzly deaths.

"An unhappy wife is a wine merchant's best friend."
—CERSEI LANNISTER

RECIPE

INGREDIENTS

1 bottle of chilled red
  wine (fruity varieties
  like Pinot Noir work
  best if you can't get
  your hands on Arbor
  Gold)
Freshly squeezed
  orange juice to taste
1 oz orange liqueur
1–2 tablespoons sugar
  or maple syrup
1 orange
1 lemon
Ice

METHOD

1 Thinly slice the orange and lemon
  and add to an ice-filled pitcher.

2 Add orange juice and sugar to taste,
  then stir until the granules are
  dissolved.

3 Add the red wine and liqueur, and
  stir.

4 Serve cold, with a side of sneer and
  a dash of withering insult.

BAR SNACK: LITTLE FINGER SANDWICHES

PLACED IN charge of both its banks and, perhaps more importantly, its brothels, Petyr Baelish was quite possibly the most powerful man in King's Landing for a while. But Littlefinger is much more than just the Master of Coin and an excuse for HBO to serve up some gratuitous nudity – even if he is just a dressing robe short of becoming the Seven Kingdoms' Hugh Hefner.

A backstabber of the highest order, he's a stealthy schemer with boundless ambition and an unhealthy obsession with the Stark women that borders on stalker territory. Above all, he's an arch gossip; the kind of man whose mouth only opens to manoeuvre people like pieces on a chessboard. With so much to do and so little time, we're sure that Lord Baelish doesn't have time for a proper sit-down meal, especially now that he's had his throat slashed by Arya Stark. Which is why we cooked up these Little Finger sandwiches, bite-sized morsels that are anything but a mouthful.

RECITE

INGREDIENTS

Bread
Your fillings of choice
(cucumber, salmon,
egg salad and chicken
salad all work well)

METHOD

1 Slice the bread.

2 Add the fillings.

3 Cut into dainty slices.

4 Realize that while we've been
giving you instructions on how
to make a simple sandwich,
Littlefinger has been secretly
plotting your downfall.

*"Money buys a man's silence
for a time, but a plateful of
sandwiches buys it forever."*
—PETYR BAELISH

SEASON 7 DRINKING GAME

Z OMBIE DRAGONS, celebrity cameos and Cersei sneering – Season 7 of *Game of Thrones* might be shorter than we're used to, but it still packs in plenty of action. There's some epic scenes, some awful moments *cough* Ed Sheeran *cough* and some plot holes that are so big you could march an army of the undead through them (just how fast can ravens fly from the Wall to Dragonstone anyway?).

But don't worry: a few drinks will help you forget all about the plot points that don't quite add up, and a lot of drinks will even help them make sense!

"A long and bloody tale. To be honest, I was drunk for most of it."
—TYRION LANNISTER

RULES

 If a character on screen drinks, you drink. Have mercy on us, Cersei!

 Take a sip every time
- Littlefinger schemes.
- a journey that would have taken an entire season to finish earlier in the show's run is completed in the space of a single scene.
- Euron Greyjoy acts like a knock-off Jack Sparrow.
- Theon gets kicked in the balls, or, you know, whatever he has going on down there now.

Finish your drink if
- there's a Stark family reunion. Include bastards and wards for extra points.
- someone says "bend the knee".

Drink for the duration when
- Ed Sheeran is on screen. I mean, who thought that it was a good idea?

Down a shot every time
- there's a Zombie dragon!
- Cersei lies, or you suspect her of lying, or she's telling the truth but you still think she's probably lying.

SEASON

8

STRAWBERRY DOTHRAKI

THE HAIR-BRAIDED, heart-eating, horse lords of Essos have been wowing fans ever since *Game of Thrones* first entered the public consciousness. Famed for their ferociousness and their ability to throw a good party – it's said that a Dothraki wedding without at least three deaths is considered a dull affair – they've played a crucial role in the battle for the Iron Throne over the past decade or so.

Sadly, much of Daenerys's Khalasar went out in a blaze of glory as the vanguard in the Battle of Winterfell. Nevertheless, Khal Drogo and co. will live long in our memories, unless you kill off your brain cells with a few too many of these moreish cocktails. It's a tasty tipple that's as red as the blood of a raw stallion's heart, as refreshing as a cool breeze on the Dothraki Sea and much tastier than the fermented mare's milk that's their usual poison of choice.

RECIPE

INGREDIENTS

18 oz strawberries
7 oz ice
3 oz rum
Juice of 1/2 a lime
Strawberry, to garnish

METHOD

1 Remove the stems from the strawberries (use an Arakh if you have one to hand) and chuck them into a blender.

2 Push the mushed-up mixture through a sieve to remove the seeds, then return it to the blender along with the ice, rum and lime juice.

3 Mix thoroughly, then pour into chilled martini glasses.

4 Garnish with strawberries, on cocktail sticks if you like.

"Iddelat."

—DOTHRAKI FOR "WELCOME" OR "DRINK"

THE WHITE
(JOHNNY) WALKER

HANGOVERS DON'T belong in a book like this. The mere mention of them is about as welcome as a takeout coffee cup on a Winterfell banquet table. But the sad truth is that if you overindulge in the contents of this cocktail compendium, you will suffer from a headache worse than Ned Stark's.

It's not just the splitting head you have to worry about either. Whether it's the groaning and sluggish movement or the zombie-like shuffle from your bed to the sofa the next morning, a cocktail hangover will turn you into the equivalent of one of the Night King's minions. But don't worry: we have a plan – one that's been more carefully laid out than the defences of the Battle of Winterfell – and that plan involves even more booze. Hair of the direwolf is just what you need to return to the living, and what better tipple to turn to than one that is aptly based on the infamous Corpse Reviver?

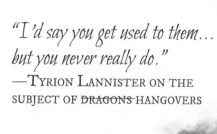

"I'd say you get used to them... but you never really do."
—TYRION LANNISTER ON THE SUBJECT OF ~~DRAGONS~~ HANGOVERS

RECIPE

INGREDIENTS

2 oz cognac
1 oz apple brandy or
Calvados
1 oz sweet vermouth
Lemon peel, to garnish

METHOD

1 Mix all of the ingredients along with ice in a cocktail shaker.

2 Strain into a chilled cocktail glass.

3 Garnish with a twist of lemon peel and enjoy, safe in the knowledge that your hangover will dissipate faster than a wight stabbed with dragonglass.

THE DRINK THAT WAS PROMISED

*G*AME OF *T*HRONES is to prophecies what a happy hour is to cocktail drinkers. In fact, the world of Westeros and beyond is jam-packed with all manner of prophecies, from the breaking of wheels to the destruction of the Red Keep. But the one prophecy that kept fans guessing right up until the end was that of Azor Ahai, or the "Prince that was Promised". The problem is that High Valyrian is notoriously tricky to translate, so much so that the words might not even mean "Prince" or "Princess" – they could even mean "the last hero".

But we think we've cracked the true meaning behind Melisandre's favourite riddle. A quick glance at our High Valyrian phrasebook tells us that Azor Ahai is not a legendary hero, but a legendary drink! Yes, we're talking about the Drink that was Promised. A cocktail that was born in salt and smoke, under a bleeding star. A cocktail that brings together fire and ice. A cocktail that will rise up and save us all from the darkness, or at the very least taste good and get you really, REALLY drunk!

RECIPE

INGREDIENTS

2 oz vodka
¾ oz orange liqueur
¾ oz fresh lime juice

"Prophecy is like a half-trained mule. It looks as though it might be useful, but the moment you trust in it, it kicks you in the head."

—TYRION LANNISTER

METHOD

1 Add all of the ingredients into a cocktail shaker with ice and mix thoroughly.

2 Strain the mixture into a chilled shot glass.

3 Drink in one go, rinse, repeat and, after a few rounds, attempt to decide who *Game of Thrones'* Azor Ahai really was.

MORMINT JULEP

THE MORMONT's are the owners of one of the most tragic Houses in *Game of Thrones*, but they're also one of the most loved. From the noble, lovelorn figure of Ser Jorah to the honourable Lord Commander Jeor – who, lest we forget, gave Jon Snow his Valyrian-steel longsword – the Bear Islanders have gifted us with some of the greatest moments in *Game of Thrones* history.

Even in a House that has provided us with so many fist-pumpingly great moments throughout the show's eight-season run, little Lady Lyanna stands out as something special. She was nothing short of a badass; a pint-sized political mastermind who died a hero's death during the Battle of Winterfell, downing a zombie giant in the process. That's why we named this cocktail in her honour – a drink that, like Lady Lyanna, packs plenty of punch despite its diminutive stature.

"We are not a large House, but we are a proud one, and every man from Bear Island drinks with the strength of ten mainlanders."
—LADY LYANNA MORMONT

RECIPE

INGREDIENTS

4–5 mint sprigs (leaves only)
1/2 oz simple syrup
2 1/2 oz bourbon
Mint sprig, to garnish.

METHOD

1 Place the mint leaves and syrup into a julep cup if you have one (a highball will do just as well if you don't).

2 Muddle thoroughly to combine the ingredients and release the oils from the mint leaves.

3 Add the bourbon.

4 Fill to the brim with crushed ice and stir until the side of the glass is as frosty as a White Walker's heart.

5 Serve with a straw and mint sprig to garnish.

GIANT'S MILK

DORNE HAS its reds, the Arbor is famed for its golds and anyone who's visited Tyrosh will tell you that its pepperwines are to die for. For those looking to scratch their alcoholic itch in the vast expanse north of the Wall, a flagon of Giant's Milk will be your tipple of choice. Like Tormund Giantsbane – a man for whom downing a flagon of ale is nothing more than merely whetting his lips (and soaking his beard) – this drink grew up to be big and strong and, thanks to our recipe, it also happens to taste absolutely delicious.

Perfect for swilling with friends in the aftermath of an epic battle, this dose of deliciousness is best served with hearty bear hugs, tall tales and demeaning jokes about Jon Snow's pecker.

"They call me Giantsbane. Want to know why? I killed a giant when I was ten. Then I climbed right into bed with his wife. When she woke up, you know what she did? Suckled me at her teat, for three months. Thought I was her baby. That's how I got so strong: giant's milk."

—TORMUND GIANTSBANE

RECIPE

INGREDIENTS

2 oz vodka
1 oz coffee cream
   liqueur
Cream to taste
Ice

METHOD

1 Fill a cocktail shaker with ice.

2 Pour vodka and coffee cream
   liqueur into the cocktail shaker.
   Mix vigorously until the surface of
   the shaker feels as cold as the Night
   King's heart.

3 Pour the alcohol into a tall glass,
   then top with cream.

4 Stir, add ice and enjoy.

THE CLEGANEBOWL

THE ONLY thing more amazing than the on-screen action you get with a smash-hit fantasy series that boasts millions of fans across the globe is the off-screen theories those millions of fans cook up online. From long-winded explanations of who will sit on the Iron Throne to detailed analyses of Jon Snow's genetic lineage, via some truly questionable erotica – we're looking at you, reddit! – *Game of Thrones* watchers have certainly played their part during the show's eight-season run.

And we can't talk about fan theories without mentioning Cleganebowl, the much-hyped showdown between brothers Sandor (the Hound) and Gregor (the Mountain) that had built ever since we learned how the Hound got his fear of fire – not to mention those facial scars. In honour of the show's squabbling siblings, we've put together a gargantuan refreshment – an eye-gougingly good take on a classic tiki cocktail that will skewer your senses. And, unlike one of Gregor's childhood toys, this drink is made to be shared.

"How can a man not keep ale in his home?"
—SANDOR "THE HOUND" CLEGANE

RECIPE

INGREDIENTS

For the drink

8 oz guava juice
8 oz pineapple juice
4 oz passionfruit juice
2 oz lemon juice
4 oz dark rum
4 oz white rum
2 oz gin
2 oz vodka
1 oz grenadine
3 cups crushed ice
6 maraschino cherries
6 pineapple chunks
Orange slices

For the flaming lime garnish

1/2 a lime
2 oz 151 proof rum

METHOD

1 Combine the guava juice, pineapple juice, passionfruit juice, dark rum, white rum, gin, lemon juice, vodka, grenadine and one cup of ice into a blender and mix it up like a decades-long feud between two burly brothers-in-arms.

2 Pour the mixture into your favourite punch bowl, along with the remaining ice, cherries, pineapple chunks and orange slices.

3 To create your flaming lime, cut your citrus fruit in half and float it on top of your cocktail. Pour a splash of overproof rum on it and carefully light with a match or lighter.

4 Serve with straws so you can drink this mountain of a drink with your friends. Just make sure you extinguish the flame first, unless you want to end up with a story that rivals Sandor's.

BRAN-DY
ALEXANDER

FROM WATCHING women birth smoke monsters to hordes of undead zombies, there's more than enough weird to go round in the world of *Game of Thrones*. And yet, for a show that thrives on strangeness, there is one character who stands head and shoulders (or should that be beak and wings?) above his contemporaries.

We are talking about Bran Stark, the young prince turned Three-Eyed Raven turned king, who has undergone one of the most extreme transformations during the current age of Westerosi history. That's why we've named this take on a classic cocktail in his honour – a delicious dose of dessert in a glass that will leave you staring creepily into the middle distance, and floor you faster than a shove out of a Winterfell window.

RECIPE

INGREDIENTS

1 1/2 oz cognac
1 oz dark crème de cacao
1 oz cream
Nutmeg, to garnish

METHOD

1 Combine all of the ingredients into a cocktail shaker with ice and, like the various strands of Westerosi history, mix thoroughly.

2 Strain into a chilled glass.

3 Garnish with nutmeg to create a drink that's guaranteed to roll your eyeballs quicker than you can say "warg".

"Old stories are like old friends. You have to visit them from time to time."
—Bran Stark

BAR SNACK: TYRIONION RINGS

You'll find plenty of pages in honour of Tyrion Lannister in this tome of tipples, and for good reason. What he lacks in stature, he more than makes up for in drunkenness, debauchery and wit so dry it's flakier than a Stone Man's scalp.

But for all his faults – and there are plenty of them – Tyrion spends the duration of the show not only trying to better himself, but better the lives of those around him. It's enough to bring tears to your eyes. Either that or someone's chopping onions in here. Oh, right...

"I would gladly give my life to watch you all swallow it!"
—Tyrion Lannister

RECIPE

INGREDIENTS

1 large onion
5 1/2 oz self-raising flour
10 oz sparkling water
Oil for frying

METHOD

1 Slice the onion, then separate the slices into rings.

2 Fill about 1/3 of a heavy-bottomed pan with oil and heat to 350° F (180 °C).

3 While the oil is heating, combine the flour and sparkling water in a bowl and mix thoroughly.

4 Dip the onion rings in the batter mixture then, using a slotted spoon, carefully lower them into the oil.

5 Cook for 2–3 minutes, or until the rings turn as golden as the contents of a Lannister's purse.

SEASON 8 DRINKING GAME

A ND NOW your watch is almost over but, before it is, you've got one final task to complete. Yes, it's time to stagger drunkenly through the events of the HBO epic one last time. Who will sit on the Iron Throne? How will they defeat the Night King? Will the writing get any better? All of these questions and much, much more will be answered over the course of the coming episodes.

So grab a drink – or even better, a handful of them – and get ready to endure / enjoy the on-screen action with our alcoholic accompaniment.

"Let's play a drinking game…"
—Tyrion
Lannister

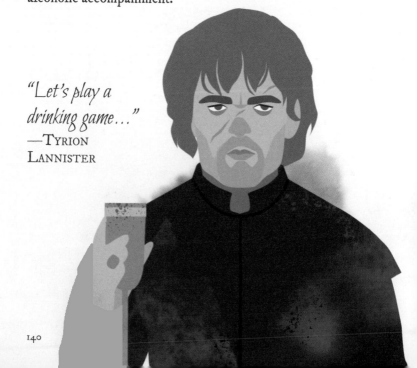

RULES

 If you don't like how the show ends, make every cocktail in this book and drink them until you forget it ever happened.

 Take a sip every time
- a dragon burns someone, or something, to a crisp.
- Tormund looks longingly at Brienne. Take two if he asks about her.
- there's a knowing callback to a previous episode.

 Finish your drink if
- a character's story arc makes no sense. Be warned: depending on how you viewed the final outing, this could floor you faster than a Valyrian dagger.
- Lyanna Mormont does something awesome.
- someone says "Dracarys".

 Drink for the duration when
- a character is writing something on screen. Perhaps the pen really is mightier than the sword?

🍶 **Down a shot every time**
- something happens that you think George R. R. Martin would have written better.
- you see something out of place – say an errant Starbucks cup or discarded water bottle.
- a major character dies – don't worry: the plot armour in this one is thicker than dragon hide.

GLOSSARY

EQUIPMENT

Highball glass – Perfect for long refreshing drinks, the highball glass is like a classic tumbler, only taller. If the Cleganes made glassware, it would almost certainly be this.

Old Fashioned glass – Named after the classic cocktail, Old Fashioned glasses are short and heavy.

Cocktail glass – Or a "martini glass", if you will. This V-shaped receptacle is perfect for drinks that are shaken, stirred and even Lannistirred.

Dragonglass – A kind of obsidian that's abundantly available on Dragonstone, this is handy to have on hand in case a White Walker interrupts your drinking session.

Flute – A classic piece of glassware that's tailor-made for champagne cocktails.

Cocktail shaker – An essential piece of equipment that does exactly what it says on the tin. If it helps, think of it as a form of exercise. That way, you can drink without ever feeling bad about yourself.

Blender – A mechanical doohickey that will slice up ingredients quicker than a Braavosi Water Dancer.

Strainer – We're not talking about the kind of straining you put your eyes through in an effort to see through all of that fog at the Battle of Winterfell. Instead, this is like a sieve, but for drinks. Simple, right?

Measuring cups / spoons – Devices that are essential for ensuring you get the right amount of booze in your cocktail. An optional extra if you want to get drunker than an imp at his own wedding ceremony.

Valyrian steel – The finest blades in all the Seven Kingdoms (and beyond). Perfect for everything from killing wights to lopping off arms.

Pitcher – A large receptacle that's perfect for storing party-sized portions of hooch. Or, if you're Cersei Lannister, a glass for one.